Table of Contents

	Page
1. Executive Summary	1
2. Strategic Vision	3
3. The Strategy	3
4. The Problem	5
5. Approaches and Findings	6
6. Recommendations and Overview of the High Pay-off Initiatives	10
7. Barriers and Mitigation Strategies	11
8. Implementation	12
9. Governance and Management of Change	18
10. Initiative Relationship to the President's Management Agenda	20

Appendices:

	Page
A. Memo From Mitchell E. Daniels, Director, Office of Management and Budget	22
B. E-Government Task Force Members	24
C. Task Force Process	25
D. Initiative Summaries	26

1. Executive Summary

We live in an increasingly interconnected society, where the Internet has spawned tremendous improvements in efficiency and customer service. People use the telephone and the Internet to get service 24 hours a day, seven days a week.

More than 60 percent of all Internet users interact with government websites. E-Government will save taxpayers a significant amount of money, while adding value to citizens' experience with government and better serving their needs. Consequently, the President has made "Expanding E-Government" integral to a five-part Management Agenda for making government more focused on citizens and results.

Federal information technology (IT) spending in the United States will exceed $48 billion in 2002 and $52 billion in 2003. That level of IT spending provides enormous opportunities for making the transformation government into a citizen-centered E-Government. Indeed, a good portion of current federal IT spending is devoted to Internet initiatives, yielding over 35 million web pages online at over 22,000 web sites. But past agency-centered IT approaches have limited the government's productivity gains and ability to serve citizens. As highlighted in this report, the federal government is poised to transform the way it does business with citizens federal government check budget through the use of E-Government.

This report presents the federal government's action plan for E-Government. The primary goals for the President's "Expanding E-Government" initiative are to:

- Make it easy for citizens to obtain service and interact with the federal government;
- Improve government efficiency and effectiveness; and
- Improve government's responsiveness to citizens.

OMB Director Mitchell E. Daniels initiated an interagency E-Government Task Force (see Appendix A) to identify the action plan for implementing the President's E-Government initiative. Under the leadership of Mark Forman, Associate Director of Information Technology and E-Government, about 80 federal employees from across the federal government made up the Task Force (see Appendix B).

The E-Government Task Force found that the federal government could significantly improve customer service over the next 18 to 24 months by focusing on 23 high-payoff, government-wide initiatives that integrate agency operations and IT investments (subsequently, payroll processing was added as the 24th E-Government initiative). These initiatives could generate several billion dollars in savings by reducing operating inefficiencies, redundant spending and excessive paperwork. The initiatives will provide service to citizens in minutes or hours, compared to today's standard of days or weeks. Moreover, by leveraging IT spending across federal agencies, the initiatives will make available over $1 billion in savings from aligning redundant investments.

The E-Government Task Force identified significant federal performance problems that could be addressed by E-Government and E-Business concepts. The Task Force's analysis found that redundant and overlapping agency activities have been major impediments to creating a citizen-centered electronic government. Of 28 lines of business found in the federal government, the assessment revealed that, on average, 19 Executive Departments and agencies are performing each line of business (see Figure 5.1). Each agency typically has invested in both online and traditional approaches, regardless of other departments' redundant efforts. That translates into many duplicative reporting requirements, while requiring citizens to wade through thousands of Web sites and dozens of call centers to find and obtain service. For example, a community attempting to obtain economic development grants could file over 1,000 forms at more than 250 federal bureaus, each form containing much similar data. The Task Force found that this "business architecture" problem creates underlying redundant activities and processes, resulting in unnecessary burdens and costs on citizens, state and local governments, businesses and federal employees.

Indeed, the Task Force found a number of unofficial groupings of federal employees who meet frequently to figure out ways to work together across traditional agency boundaries and better serve citizens. Through e-mails and interviews, the Task Force found that many government employees want to use E-Government tools that enable teamwork in their daily work.

The Task Force also identified key barriers that must be mitigated for success in federal E-Government efforts. The barriers identified concerned culture, architecture, trust, resources and stakeholder resistance. Several recommendations for leadership actions were made to overcome these barriers. In addition, two efforts—the e-Authentication initiative and the Enterprise E-Government Architecture Project—were added to address key barriers.

- The e-Authentication initiative will build and enable mutual trust to support wide spread use of electronic interactions between the public and government and across government by providing common solutions to establish 'identity'. These solutions will address authentication security, privacy, and electronic signature needs of the E-Government initiatives.

- The E-Government Architecture project will carry out two major concurrent activities. One of the activities will be the development of a architecture, toward the development of a Federal Enterprise Architecture, for each of the current E-Government initiatives, as well as a core set of standardized technology models to facilitate technology solutions. The second activity will be the collection and analysis of business and data architecture information across the federal government to identify new opportunities for E-Government initiatives and elimination of redundancy. Initially this effort will focus on four key areas including Homeland Security, economic stimulus, social services, and back office operations.

The President's Management Council approved the E-government initiatives and the action plan in their October 3, 2001, meeting. Through December 2001, agencies developed detailed business cases and formed partnerships for investment and implementation of the initiatives.

The results of the business cases were incorporated into the Fiscal Year 2003 budget, and agencies are currently integrating planned FY 2002 efforts into the 24 E-Government initiatives.

Information on this E-government effort may be found on the Internet at, http://www.firstgov.gov, http://www.whitehouse.gov/OMB, or http://www.cio.gov, including an electronic copy of this report.

2. STRATEGIC VISION

The President's vision for reforming government emphasizes that "government needs to reform its operations—how it goes about its business and how it treats the people it serves." The vision is guided by three principles:

- **Citizen-centered,** not bureaucracy-centered;
- **Results-oriented;** and
- **Market-based**, actively promoting innovation.

Electronic government is one of the five key elements in the President's Management Agenda and Performance Plan (August 2001) for achieving the vision. E-Government is critical to meeting today's citizen and business expectations for interaction with government. It will enable agencies to align efforts as needed to significantly improve service and reduce operating costs. When E-Government initiatives deploy effectively, conducting business with the government is easier, privacy is protected and security provided. Citizens and businesses can visit one point-of-service online or by telephone that reflects the "United States Government."

Our vision combines successful online operating practices with the federal government's human capital and physical assets to build a "click and mortar" enterprise. In this vision, organizations serve citizens, businesses, other government and federal employees. Our goal is that services and information will rarely be more than three clicks away when using the Internet. Achieving this vision requires that agencies integrate and simplify their operations.

3. THE STRATEGY

The Administration is committed to advancing the E-Government strategy by supporting multi-agency projects that improve citizen services and yield performance gains. With that objective, the Task Force developed a roadmap for the implementation of E-Government. OMB Director Mitchell E. Daniels initiated an interagency E-Government Task Force (see Appendix A) to identify the action plan for implementing the President's E-Government initiative. The Task Force's objectives were to:

- Recommend highest payoff cross-agency initiatives that can be rapidly developed;

- Identify key barriers to the federal government becoming a citizen-centered E-Government, and implement actions needed to overcome these barriers; and
- Develop a technology framework that provides for the integration of government services and information.

What is the value of E-Government?

E-Government provides many opportunities to improve the quality service to the citizen. Citizens should be able to get service or information in minutes or hours, versus today's standard of days or weeks. Citizens, businesses and state and local governments should be able to file required reports without having to hire accountants and lawyers. Government employees should be able to do their work as easily, efficiently and effectively as their counterparts in the commercial world.

An effective strategy will result in significant improvements in the federal government, including:

- Simplifying delivery of services to citizens;
- Eliminating layers of government management;
- Making it possible for citizens, businesses, other levels of government and federal employees to easily find information and get service from the federal government;
- Simplifying agencies' business processes and reducing costs through integrating and eliminating redundant systems;
- Enabling achievement of the other elements of the President's Management Agenda; and
- Streamlining government operations to guarantee rapid response to citizen needs.

This focuses on four citizen-centered groups, each providing opportunities to transform delivery of services.

- Individuals/Citizens: Government-to-Citizens (G2C); Build easy to find, easy to use, one-stop points-of-service that make it easy for citizens to access high-quality government services.
- Businesses: Government-to-Business (G2B); Reduce government's burden on businesses by eliminating redundant collection of data and better leveraging E-business technologies for communication.
- Intergovernmental: Government-to-Government (G2G); Make it easier for states and localities to meet reporting requirements and participate as full partners with the federal government in citizen services, while enabling better performance measurement, especially for grants. Other levels of government will see significant administrative savings and will be able to improve program delivery because more accurate data is available in a timely fashion.
- Intra-governmental: Internal Efficiency and Effectiveness (IEE); Make better use of modern technology to reduce costs and improve quality of federal government agency administration, by using industry best practices in areas such as supply-chain management, financial management and knowledge management. Agencies will be able to improve

effectiveness and efficiency, eliminating delays in processing and improving employee satisfaction and retention.

4. THE PROBLEM

While the federal government is the world's biggest spender on information technology, it has not experienced commensurate improvements in productivity, quality and customer service. In many companies, major gains have come from leveraging the technology to transform old business practices. There are at least four major reasons that the federal government has been unable to increase productivity:

- **Program Performance Value**: Agencies typically evaluate their IT systems according to how well they serve the agency's processes and needs—not how well they respond to citizens' needs. Systems are often evaluated by the percentage of time they are working, rather than the internal and external performance benefit they deliver to the programs they support.
- **Technology Leverage**: In the 1990s, government agencies used IT to automate existing processes, rather than to create more efficient and effective solutions that are now possible because of commercial E-business lessons learned.
- **Islands of Automation**: Agencies generally buy systems that address internal needs, and rarely are the systems able to inter-operate or communicate with those in other agencies. Consequently, citizens have to search across multiple agencies to get service, businesses have to file the same information multiple times, and agencies cannot easily share information.
- **Resistance to Change**: Budget processes and agency cultures perpetuate obsolete bureaucratic divisions. Budgeting processes have not provided a mechanism for investing in cross-agency IT. Moreover, agency cultures and fear of reorganization create resistance to integrating work and sharing use of systems across several agencies.

Better leveraging technology investments will require that government managers look beyond the current ways of doing work. Today's IT solutions incorporate more productive ways of doing work, either through eliminating paperwork or integrating activities across longstanding organizational silos. Consequently, affected program officials need to be involved in strategic IT investment decisions. These investments need to be based on valid business cases that clearly articulate the value to both the citizen and the government, and provide for privacy and security that is critical to successful e-government.

A fundamental barrier to getting productivity from federal government IT is government's inherent resistance to change. E-Government uses IT to improve federal productivity by enabling better interactions and coordination. But each opportunity requires substantial changes in current bureaucratic procedures. Success will depend on breaking down the resistance to such change. A holistic approach is needed, and each E-Government initiative must include results oriented performance measures, policy alignment, training, communications, and organizational change milestones.

5. APPROACH AND FINDINGS

Overview

The E-Government Task Force conducted 71 interviews with more than 150 senior government officials during the process to gather and identify strategic E-Government opportunities (See Appendix C). In addition, nearly 200 projects were identified from e-mails sent primarily by federal employees. The overall findings were that agency executives and line professionals want the government to:

- Use the Web to provide services such as benefits, recreational opportunities, and educational materials;
- Share information and integrate federal, state and local data where appropriate and possible;
- Reduce burden on businesses by adopting streamlined processes that promote and enable consolidation in data collection;
- Adopt commercial best practices to reduce operating costs and make it simpler for government employees to perform their jobs, especially in the areas of finance, human resources and procurement; and
- Define measures of success and regularly monitor and measure performance.

Reducing Overlap and Redundancy to Make It Easier for Citizens to Get Service and to Reduce Costs

One of the most significant findings of the Task Force came from a review of the federal government's enterprise architecture. An enterprise architecture describes how an organization performs its work using people, business processes, data, and technology. Since E-Government opportunities affect how agencies do their work and employ technology, it was necessary to evaluate the projects identified against the current enterprise architecture. The assessment applied the approach of the Federal Chief Information Officers Council, using the enterprise architecture to establish a "roadmap to achieve an agency's mission through optimal performance of its core business processes within an efficient IT environment." The Task Force began the assessment by creating a clear framework of the federal government's business architecture, detailing how the federal government interfaces with citizens, what functions and lines of business the government performs and the key business processes used.

The Task Force's major finding was that there was significant overlap and redundancy, with multiple agencies performing each of 30 major functions and business lines in the Executive Branch of government. The review clearly identified the current federal enterprise architecture as "the architecture that isn't". The final analysis indicated that each line of business is being performed by 19 agencies (average) and that each agency is involved in 17 business lines (average) (See figure 5.1). The Task Force found that this "business architecture" redundancy creates excessive duplicative spending on staff, IT and administration. Moreover, the Task Force assessment determined that the redundancy makes it hard to get service, while generating duplicative reporting and paperwork burdens. Consequently, the Task Force focused on E-Government initiatives that provide significant opportunities to transform the way the government interacts with its citizens, through the elimination of redundancy and creating simpler ways for citizens to get service.

As the Task Force evaluated potential projects relative to the business architecture, the assessment focused on the opportunities to integrate operations and simplify processes within a line of business across agencies and around citizen needs. Activities of the federal government can be viewed in four primary functions: policymaking, program administration, compliance, and enforcement and internal operations and infrastructure. Policy making activities generally determine programs and compliance efforts. Internal operations are administrative functions, such as financial management, that support day-to-day activities needed to carry out policy making, program administration and compliance activities. E-Government offers the opportunity to streamline activities, improving productivity by enabling agencies to focus on their core competencies and mission requirements. E-Government initiatives eliminate unnecessary redundancy, while improving service quality by simplifying processes and unifying agency islands of automation.

Figure 5.1: *Agency Activity on Lines of Business Across Government*

Data compiled for Agency's Budget Exhibits and Agency Websites (this is not intended as a full accounting)

Columns (Lines of Business): Econ. Dev. | Nat'l Sec, Def, & Ops | Regulation Creation | Public Safety | Diplomacy | Disaster Prep. & Response Mgmt | Energy Production | Asset Mgt. | Permits & Licensing | Grants & Loans | Transportation | Insurance | Consumer Protect | Social Services | Accounts Payable and Receivable | Rec & Nat'l Res | R&D Science | Import / Exports | Environm'l Mgmt | Labor | Regulation Compl | Tax Collection | HR | Finance | Procurement | Travel | Logistics | Admin | Total

Agencies (rows): AF, AR, DefAg, DOC, DOE, DOI, DOJ, DOL, DOS, DOT, Ed, EPA, FEMA, FCC, FTC, FRB, GSA, HHS, HUD, NASA, NAVY, NRC, NSF, OPM, SBA, SSA, Treas, USAID, USDA, VA

Column totals: 24 | 10 | 29 | 21 | 3 | 31 | 4 | 29 | 16 (21) | 2 | 7 | 8 | 14 | 30 | 7 | 11 | 6 | 22 | 6 | 30 | 2 | 30 | 30 | 30 | 30 | 30 | 30 | 30 | Total: 495

8.

An Integrated Government-wide Business Architecture

Access Channels							
Web Services	Telephone - Voice - Interactive	E-system to System	Private/Public Partnerships	Face to Face	Fax	Kiosks	Mail

Lines of Business

Policy Making	Program Admin	Compliance
Disaster Preparedness Economic Development National Security, Foreign Relations & Defense Public Safety Regulatory – Creation	Asset Mgmt Defense & Nat'l Security Ops Diplomacy Disaster Response Management Energy Production Grants/Loans Insurance Permits/Licensing Social Services: Monetary Benefits, In-kind (Health, Nutrition, & Housing), Education Recreation & Natural Resources R&D & Science	Consumer Safety Environment Mgmt Labor Law Enforcement Other Regulatory Compliance (e.g., Communications) Tax Collection Trade (Import/Export) Transportation

Internal Operations / Infrastructure
HR – Finance (GL/AP/AR) — Travel – Supply Chain Mgmt (Procurement/Inventory Cntl/Logistics) – Admin

Underlying Processes / Value Chains

Information Value Chain:	Capture ⟹ Store ⟹ Query ⟹ Distribute ⟹ Analyze ⟹ Act ⟹ Learn
Supply Chain Mgt:	Order ⟹ Capture ⟹ Fulfill

Command and Control: evolving

Figure: 5.2: *The Business Architecture*

Prioritizing Initiatives

The 24 E-Government initiatives were selected using two rounds of prioritization. Overlaying the 350 plus projects that the taskforce gathered from the interviews and e-mails against the architecture assessment yielded 30 potential E-Government initiatives. The most promising initiatives were selected on the basis of value to citizens, potential improvement in agency efficiency and likelihood of deploying within 18 to 24 months.

Initial business cases were developed for each of the 30 initiatives, yielding estimates of benefits, costs and risks. Twenty-four of the 30 would derive significant benefits from simplifying the underlying processes, and 17 of the 30 would derive significant benefits from unifying infrastructure and operations across agency silos. Overall, the 30 initiatives provide an opportunity to improve response to citizens by an order of magnitude (e.g. days instead of weeks). They provide the opportunity to better use billions of dollars in redundant IT investment and operating costs. They could reduce government's burden on citizens, businesses and state and local governments by well over a billion dollars. Using this data from the business cases, the 20 most promising initiatives were recommended for deployment, with initiatives addressing each citizen-centered group (citizens, businesses, state and local governments and internal efficiency and effectiveness). In addition, two initiatives were selected for further business case development: healthcare informatics and e-Vital. Finally, e-Authentication was selected to address the authentication security needs that cut across federal E-Government initiatives.

The selections were made by a steering group comprised of the members of the President's Management Council under the leadership of the OMB Director. The full President's Management Council approved 23 initiatives at the October 3, 2001 meeting. Subsequently, payroll processing was added as the 24th initiative.

Figure 5.3 *Summary of E-Government Portfolios*

G2C	G2B
• Use the web for accessing services such as benefits, loans, recreational sites & educational material • Key lines of business: social services, recreation & natural resources, grants/loans, taxes	• Reduce burden on businesses by adopting processes that enable collecting data once for multiple uses & streamlining redundant data • Key lines of business: regulation, economic development, trade, permits/licenses, grants/loans, asset management
G2G	**IEE**
• Share & integrate federal, state & local data • Key lines of business: economic development, recreation & natural resources, public safety, law enforcement, disaster response management, grants/loans	• Adopt commercial best practices in government operation (supply chain management, HR document workflow) • Key lines of business: supply chain management, HR, finance

6. RECOMMENDATIONS AND OVERVIEW OF THE HIGH PAY-OFF INITIATIVES

The President's Management Council selected the E-Government initiatives on the basis of potential value identified in the initial business cases. The initiatives selected provide the most value to citizens, while generating cost savings or improving effectiveness of government. The 24 projects achieve these results by simplifying and unifying agency work processes and information flows, providing one-stop services to citizens and enabling information to be collected online once and reused, versus re-collected many times.

Managing partners were selected along with other agency partners to lead the new efforts. Subsequent work by the managing partners and their agency partners has yielded more detailed business cases, generally building on current related initiatives (e.g., the International Trade Process Streamlining initiative led by the Commerce Department). With the goal of realizing the business case for each initiative within 24 months, the managing partners will oversee deployment of modules for each initiative in six-month increments as modules become operational.

Additional information about the projects is available in Appendix D, Initiative Summaries.

7. BARRIERS AND MITIGATION STRATEGIES

The Task Force identified key barriers that may prevent the successful implementation of each initiative. Recurring barriers included agency culture, lack of federal architecture, trust, resources, and stakeholder resistance. The Task Force then worked with the Steering Group to define actions for overcoming the barriers. Table 7-1 lists the actions endorsed by the President's Management Council for overcoming each chronic barrier.

One barrier frequently cited is the need to ensure adequate security and privacy. A successful E-Government strategy must deploy effective security controls into government processes and systems. E-Government must also ensure privacy for personal information that is shared with the Federal Government. The e-Authentication project will enable mutual trust to support widespread use of electronic interactions between the public and government and across government by providing common solutions to establish 'identity'. It will provide a secure, easy to use and consistent method of proving identity to the federal government that is an appropriate match to the level of risk and business needs of each initiative. In addition, project teams will address privacy concerns regarding the sharing of personal information. E-government depends on confidence by citizens that the government is handling their personal information with care. Agencies are working on building strong privacy protections into the E-Government initiatives and OMB is focusing on government wide privacy protections by all agencies.

Table 7-1 *Actions for Overcoming Barriers to E-Government*

Barrier	Mitigation
Agency Culture	• Sustain high level leadership and commitment • Establish interagency governance structure • Give priority to cross-agency work • Engage interagency user/stakeholder groups, including communities of practice
Lack of Federal Architecture	• OMB leads government-wide business and data architecture rationalization • OMB sponsors architecture development for cross-agency projects • FirstGov.gov will be the primary online delivery portal for G2C and G2B interactions
Trust	• Through e-Authentication E-Government initiative, establish secure transactions and identity authentication that will be used by all E-Government initiatives • Incorporate security and privacy protections into each business plan • Provide public training and promotion
Resources	• Move resources to programs with greatest return and citizen impact • Set measures up-front and use to monitor implementation • Provide online training to create new expertise among employees/contractors
Stakeholder Resistance	• Create comprehensive strategy for engaging Congressional committees • Have multiple PMC members argue collectively for initiatives • Tie performance evaluations to cross-agency success • Communicate strategy to stakeholders

8. IMPLEMENTATON

The E-Government Management Action Plan

Today, the federal government has only scratched the surface of the E-Government potential. Most current efforts merely move decades old agency practices onto the Internet. Consequently, there are more than 35 million federal Web pages available at over 22,000 federal Web sites. While agencies have spent two years considering how to move 6,600 types of paper-based transactions online (representing millions of individual transactions per year), only hundreds are online today. Given the redundant and outdated activities inherent in the 6,600 transactions, the Task Force identified that successful E-Government implementation would have to significantly streamline interactions. The Task Force identified several hundred opportunities each requiring significant change from traditional bureaucratic approaches.

The Task Force determined that successful implementation will be difficult without prioritizing opportunities and engaging federal leaders to focus resources on initiatives that give the greatest results. Consequently, the 24 initiatives chosen represent a balance of initiatives and resources across the four key citizen groups (individuals, businesses, intergovernmental and internal). The initiatives will integrate dozens of overlapping agency E-Government projects that would have made worse the confusing array of federal Web sites. Additionally, the 24 initiatives represent the priorities of the members of the President's Management Council, who can provide the key leadership support needed to overcome resistance to change.

The 24 initiatives will be managed using a portfolio management process, which manages risk within the range of initiatives for improving service to a given citizen-centered grouping. The four portfolios and their strategic foci are:

- The Government to Citizen (G2C) initiatives will fulfill the vision of one-stop, online access to benefits, and services (such as "Recreation.gov"). They will also bring modern relationship management tools to improve the quality and efficiency of service delivery.
- The Government to Business (G2B) initiatives will reduce burden on businesses by adopting processes that dramatically reduce redundant data collection, provide one-stop streamlined support for businesses, and enable digital communication with businesses using the language of E-business (XML).
- The Government to Government (G2G) initiatives will enable sharing and integration of federal, state and local data to facilitate better leverage of investments in IT systems (e.g. geographical information) and to provide better integration of key government operations, such as disaster response. The G2G initiatives also improve grant management capabilities, as required by the Federal Financial Assistance Improvement Act (P.L 106-107). These initiatives will also support "vertical" (i.e., intergovernmental) integration requirements for Homeland Security.
- The Internal Efficiency and Effectiveness (IEE) initiatives bring commercial best practices to key government operations, particularly supply chain management, human capital management, financial management and document workflow.

Overall, the initiatives represent an opportunity to more effectively use billions of dollars of federal funds, while accelerating government response times from weeks down to minutes. In addition, the initiatives provide an opportunity to save billions of dollars currently spent by citizens, businesses and state and local governments to comply with paperwork-intensive government processes.

However, the pay-off will not result from automating current processes, but rather through the transformation of how the government interacts with its citizens and customers. Only through changing how we do business internally—that is, streamlining work processes to take advantage of modern IT systems—will citizens experience the transformation envisioned. OMB will work closely with the lead and partner agencies to establish appropriate and equitable implementation and resource plans for these initiatives.

E-Government Strategy

Figure 8-1 *Timeline for Deployment*
This is non-exhaustive list that will grow or be modified as the initiatives evolve.

Project	Milestone	Date
	Government to Citizen	
Recreation One Stop	Revised Recreation.gov deployed	Completed
	First version of Volunteer.gov online	4/31/02
	RFPs or agreements with private sector reached on implementation of new recreation online projects	TBD
	Additional recreation projects (reservations, searchable maps, more recreation information, etc.) available online	TBD
Eligibility Assistance Online	Initial release of online screening tool for 20 benefit programs	4/31/02
	Online screening tool for 100 benefit programs	9/30/02
	Targeted consolidation of online benefit application and customer relationship management	TBD
Online Access for Loans	Deploy "seek and find" methodology to make it easier for the public to find loan information	TBD
USA Services	Enable citizens to personalize the combination of services they obtain across multiple programs	TBD
	Enable a case to be created and acted upon by multiple agencies	TBD
	Implement a multi-channel contact center to facilitate easy access to information and service	TBD
EZ Tax Filing	Internet fact of filing and refund	4/31/02
	Initial deployment of industry partnership free e-filing solution for 2003 season	12/31/02
	Government to Business	
Online Rulemaking Management	Develop capability assessment of "top ten" rulemaking agencies' docket systems – who has the best existing solution	3/30/02
	Create a page, through FIRSTGOV, that links to all agency's docket sites	4/15/02
	Complete study of requirements for moving rulemaking agencies to an integrated online rulemaking system	8/30/02
	Deploy unified cross-agency public comment site	TBD
	Deploy a single on-line rulemaking dockets application to include integration with the RISC/OIRA Consolidated Information System (ROCIS)	TBD
Expanding Electronic Tax Products for Businesses	Begin deployment of filing of W2s on the internet	2/01/02
	Complete XML or non EDI formats (schemas) for electronic filing of 94x	8/31/02
	Begin deployment of the interim solution for online EIN by November 2002 (IRS)	11/31/02
	By January 2004 target initial implementation of 1120 efile for business to facilitate end to end tax administration	1/15/04

14.

Federal Asset Sales	Re-host Federal Sales	3/31/02
	Develop pilot business integration	9/30/02
	Pilot transaction platform	3/31/03
International Trade Process Streamlining	Complete EX-IM Working Capital Automation Project and Integrate into Export.gov	4/15/02
	Deploy on-line collaborative workspace that consolidates all of the information gathering by trade specialists and disseminates it through export.gov to SMEs.	8/15/02
	Simplify EX-IM Insurance filing processes and products and integrate them into Export.gov	1/15/03
One-Stop Business Compliance Information	Pilot/test prototype content management tool for Businesslaw.gov. Conduct full inventory/registry of regulatory agency's "plain language" compliance assistance tools	8/1/02
	Prototype seamless intergovernmental licensing and permitting tool to include Internet EIN	11/30/02
	Complete 30 expert tools (from multiple agencies to include OSHA, EPA, IRS, INS, DOT, DOE) designed to help businesses to comply with relevant regulations in the environment, health and safety, employment, and taxes.	5/1/03

Government to Government

Geospatial Information One-Stop	Complete draft standards for critical spatial data themes (framework data)	9/30/02
	Identify Federal inventories of framework data	9/30/02
	Deploy first iteration of the Geospatial One-Stop	TBD
e-Grants	Finalize the E-Grants business case in support of partner requirements and other participant input	4/15/02
	Evaluate the use or expansion of interagency and agency specific capabilities for discretionary grant programs	6/1/02
	Pilot a simple, unified way to find federal grant opportunities via the Web	7/1/02
	Define application data standards	10/1/02
	Deploy simple, unified grant application mechanism	10/1/03
Disaster Assistance and Crisis Response	Finalize the business case in support of partner requirements and other participant input	05/15/02
	Deploy a single portal for citizens, public and private institutions that provides access to information and services relating to Disaster and Crisis Management	TBD
Wireless Public Safety Interoperable Communications – Project SAFECOM	Define the communications concept of operations for interaction that identifies the communications requirements to address the two highest probable threat scenarios: Bio terrorism and natural disasters.	05/31/2002
	Develop an integrated public safety response solution that addresses the top two threat scenarios by using existing infrastructure augmented by available commercial capability.	09/30/02
	Complete a gap analysis of existing inventories of public safety wireless communications at federal, state, and local level.	12/31/02
	Implement Priority Wireless Access.	TBD

e-Vital	Finalize the business case in support of partner requirements and other participant input, and submit to the PMC	05/15/02
	Deploy electronic process for Federal and State agencies to collect, process, analyze, and disseminate Electronic Verification of Vital Events (EVVE) records.	TBD
	Deploy an electronic process for Federal and State agencies to collect, process, analyze, and disseminate Electronic Death Registration (EDR) records	TBD
Internal Efficiency & Effectiveness		
E-Training	Initial e-Training system operational with mandatory Government courses (module 1) -	10/15/02
	Expanded e-Training system with fee-for-service courses (Module 2)	4/30/03
	Enhanced e-Training system contains user and managerial tools (such as virtual classrooms and evaluation tools (Modules 2 and 3)	11/01/03
Recruitment One-Stop	Implement simple front-end – Improved appearance and usability that mirrors popular private sector internet recruiting sites	6/30/02
	Applicant status applicant database mining, intake of paper resumes/applications, and capability to link to Federal agency's assessment tools.	1/31/03
	Integration with agency assessment tools.	6/30/03
Integrated Human Resources	HR Logical Data Model including metadata, extended markup language (XML) tags, including proposal for standard Federal HR data	9/30/02
	Prototype Analytical Tools Enabling Integrated Resource Management, Workforce Planning, and Policy Analysis	12/31/02
	Design notional architecture for HR initiatives integration to include financial management	11/30/02
E-Clearance	Clearance Verification System which creates a common, source of investigative info to support employee assignment	12/31/02
	Implement e-QIP to reduce error rejection rate, eliminate manual data transfers	6/30/03
	Connect OPM & DoD security clearance indexes	12/31/02
e- Payroll/HR (Payroll Processing Consolidation)	Complete and submit business case to the PMC	3/31/02
	Integrated Enterprise Architecture	TBD
	Strengthening Payroll Service Delivery	TBD
e-Travel	Government wide web-based end to end solutions initial capabilities assessment (ICA)	10/01/02
	E-Travel Customer Care Implemented	12/01/02
	Web Travel Authorization and Voucher System (TAVS)	6/30/03
	Integrated Solution	12/30/03
Integrated Acquisition Environment	Integrated Vendor Profile Network – IVPN Single point of vendor registration, initial capability	6/30/02
	Consolidated eCatalog –Implement a directory of GWAC and MAC contracts to simplify selection and facilitate leverage of Government buying, initial capability	9/30/02
	Federal Acquisition Management Information System – FAMIS Implement a new web-based Federal Management Information System that is integrated with legacy systems and provides useful real-time data, initial capability	9/30/03

E-Government Strategy

Electronic Records Management	With partners, finalize ERM initiative work plan and types of ERM guidance and tools to be developed in initiative	5/31/02
	Issue first ERM guidance product (subsequent products to be identified with their timelines under the first milestone)	9/30/02
	Issue first lessons learned/best practices model	9/30/02
	Complete RM and archival XML schema	2/28/03
	Develop ERM requirements that agencies can incorporate in their system designs	04/30/03
	Issue final guidance products and tools	9/30/03
Cross Cutting Initiatives		
E-Authentication	Define operational concept including critical success factors and requirements for 12 of the projects.	7/1/02
	Initial authentication gateway prototype	9/30/02
	Full deployment	9/30/03
	Government-wide authentication guidance	TBD
Federal Enterprise Architecture	Produce a set of generally accepted, component-based technology models to guide the target and transition architectures of the currently approved E-government initiatives	3/15/02
	Identify opportunities, based upon agreed criteria measuring impact and value to the citizen, for additional e-Government initiatives (Budget Year 2003/2004)	4/30/02
	Deliver a Federal EA repository with high level business and data architecture in 4 focus areas: Homeland Security, Social Services, Economic Stimulus, and Back Office Operations	4/30/02

9. GOVERNANCE AND MANAGEMENT OF CHANGE

In implementing the Action Plan, the daily management and leadership will be provided by:

- Senior agency officials who comprise the President's Management Council;
- The Office of the Associate Director of OMB for IT and E-Government and other OMB staff;
- Members of the CIO, CFO, and Procurement Executive and Human Resources Councils.

One of the most significant barriers to successful implementation of E-government is the resistance of organizations to change. In her recent book, *Evolve*, Rosabeth Moss Kanter, noted author on the successful transformation of organizations, characterized failed, halfhearted attempts at E-business as like "putting lipstick on a bulldog". She goes on to say, "Success requires systemic change, a shift in the organizational way of life." E-Government, like E-business, is about fundamental change in the way organizations and processes work to take advantage of opportunities the technology offers.

To succeed will require an effective governance structure to overcome the barriers and implement the changes necessary. This includes substantial, long-term commitment by senior management. The Administration is using the President's Management Council (PMC) to ensure this management commitment.

PMC members volunteered to be "managing partners" for each of the initiatives. Other members volunteered to participate in those efforts as partners. The managing partners are establishing program offices to ensure that the initiatives are implemented, and the partners will cooperate in the planning and implementation of the initiative. OMB is overseeing this process and working with the agencies on adequate funding for the initiatives. Consequently, OMB has hired four Portfolio Managers, reporting to the Associate Director for IT and E-Government, who are responsible for overseeing progress in the E-Government initiatives.

The PMC will also focus on organizational and process changes across government agencies to facilitate citizen-centered transformation. As such, the Council will be a key component of governance for the transformation of the federal government to E-Government. To help this transformation, the CIO Council, with participation from the other federal management councils, will form portfolio steering groups to focus on E-Government in each of the four citizen segments: G2C, G2B, G2G, and Internal Efficiency and Effectiveness. Portfolio Steering Group members will be from agencies that make up the project teams for each of the initiatives. In addition, the G2G Steering Committee will include representation from official state and local government organizations. The steering committees will advise agency program managers concerning their initiatives and help remove barriers to the implementation of the initiatives. The Committees will also support their corresponding portfolio manager, an OMB employee who is responsible for making government more citizen-centered through daily interaction with the managing partners who they oversee.

Metrics will be used to track progress both for the agency and the cross-agency E-Government. The President's Management Council will be closely involved and track E-Government progress at its regular meetings. OMB will be working with Department and agency E-Government leaders, as well as their CIOs, to ensure success. Progress will be tracked for each E-Government initiative, and agency success and cooperation will be documented in the President's Management Agenda Scorecard.

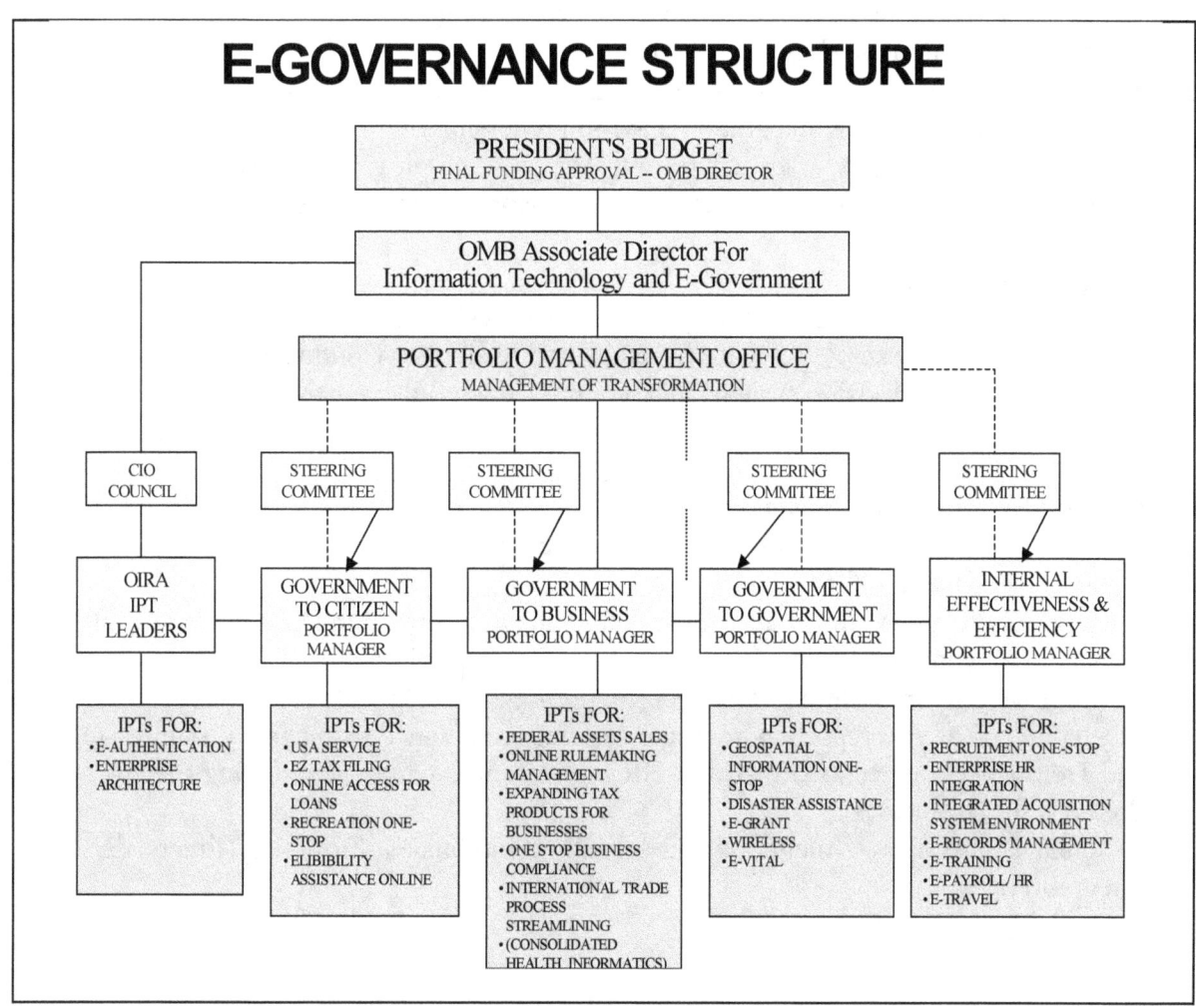

Figure 9.1 *Governance Structure*
Key to acronyms: CIO- Chief Information Officer, HR- Human Resources;
IPT Integrated Project Team

10. INITIATIVE'S RELATIONSHIP TO PRESIDENT'S MANAGEMENT AGENDA

The E-Government Task Force initiatives described in this report not only address the "Expanding E-Government" directions of the President's Management Agenda, but also are key enablers for the President's other reform initiatives. The President's Management Agenda (PMA) FY 2002 can be found at http://www.firstgov.gov, http://www.whitehouse.gov/OMB or http://www.cio.gov. Key elements of the initiatives that drive other parts of the Management Agenda are discussed below.

Strategic Management of Human Capital
- Accelerate recruitment and hiring, as well as hiring college graduates in a manner commensurate with their job search approach (Recruitment One-Stop)
- Reduce time to make better decisions (all initiatives, for example e-Training)
- Adopt IT systems to capture knowledge of retiring employees (e-Records)
- Make better use of e-Training to leverage scarce training funds and develop government-wide competencies within job skill needs (e-Training)
- Integrate commercial best practices in Enterprise Resource Management (ERP) regarding workforce (Enterprise HR Integration, Payroll Processing)
- Attract Internet savvy graduates from top schools and provide modern work environment with HR systems that facilitate employees doing their work (all initiatives)

Competitive Sourcing
- Accomplish E-government through adoption of best commercial practices and systems/implicit (all initiatives, for example Integrated Acquisition Systems/e-Contract Services)
- Use rule-based decision systems inherent in IT to facilitate outsourcing of commercial activities currently performed in-house (Business Compliance One-Stop and Federal Asset Sales)

Improved Financial Performance
- Eliminate erroneous benefit and assistance payments (Online Eligibility Assistance, e-Vital, Consolidated Health Informatics)
- Generate accurate, timely and integrated financial information (Enterprise HR Integration, Payroll Processing, Integrated Acquisition Environment, e-Grants)
- Improve timelines: Re-engineer reporting process and expand uses of Web-based processes; accelerate end of year reporting; measure systems compliance with agency's ability to meet OMB and Treasury requirements (Enterprise HR Integration, e-Grants, Expanding Electronic Tax Products for Businesses)
- Enhance usefulness: Integrate financial and performance information (Enterprise HR Integration)

Budget and Performance Integration

- Standardize integrated budgeting performance and accounting information systems at the program level to provide timely feedback for management and roll-up to government-wide view and decisions (Enterprise HR Integration as a component)
- Improve productivity focus for E-Government initiatives with new initiatives being identified in the federal architecture work

Appendix A

EXECUTIVE OFFICE OF THE PRESIDENT
OFFICE OF MANAGEMENT AND BUDGET
WASHINGTON, D.C. 20503

M-01-28

July 18, 2001

MEMORANDUM FOR THE HEADS OF EXECUTIVE DEPARTMENTS AND AGENCIES

FROM: Mitchell E. Daniels, Jr. /s/

SUBJECT: Citizen-Centered E-Government: Developing the Action Plan

Electronic government is one of the five key elements in the President's Management and Performance Plan. The President's Budget outlined how we will focus our E-Government initiatives on reforming the government so that it is citizen-centered. This memorandum describes our plan to establish a Task Force to begin implementing the President's initiative and asks for your assistance and support in these efforts.

Within our organizations, staff already know of many potential opportunities for using information technologies to improve the service we provide to citizens. Our approach, modeled on the best practices of the private sector, is to tap into that knowledge and use it to identify applications of Internet technologies to reform the way our organizations do business.

Because E-Government is at the core of the President's management agenda, I recently created the position in the Office of Management and Budget (OMB) of Associate Director for Information Technology and E-Government to lead the effort in achieving the President's E-Government vision. I have asked Mark Forman, the new Associate Director, to lead an interagency to define an action plan and road map. We ask your help in establishing this Task Force of knowledgeable individuals to identify high payoff E-Government opportunities and set in motion a transformation of government around customer needs. The Task Force will identify priority actions to achieve strategic improvements the following four areas of service:

- Service to *individuals*: deploy easy to find one-stop shops for citizens, including single points of easy entry to access high quality government services;

- Service to *businesses*: reduce burden on businesses by using Internet protocols and consolidating the myriad of redundant reporting requirements;

- *Intergovernmental affairs*: make it easier for States to meet reporting requirements, while enabling better performance measurement and results, especially for grants; and

- *Internal efficiency and effectiveness*: improve the performance and reduce costs of federal government administration by using e-business best practices in areas such as supply chain management, financial management, and knowledge management.

The Task Force will operate as an interagency working group over a period of five to six weeks, beginning later this month. I have asked Mark Forman to act as the project executive for the Task Force and report progress to me and an executive steering committee. The Task Force will be successful only if it comprises individuals knowledgeable in their agency programs and experienced in government reform initiatives.

To assist in this effort, I ask that you identify a senior E-Government leader who reports directly to you, to work with Mark in establishing the Task Force. Specific time commitments for individuals participating from your Department or agency will be determined on the basis of a discussion between your E-Government leader and Mark. Please have your Department or agency provide names and contact information for your E-Government leader to Mr. Alex Wilson (wwilson@omb.eop.gov) at 202-395-3787. If you would like more detailed information, Mark Forman can be reached at 202-395-1148.

Appendix B: Task Force Members

Agriculture:
MacDonald, Robert
Niedermayer, Chris

Central Intelligence Agency:
Reid, Jim

Commerce:
Guarguilo, John
Hogan, Karen
Lyons, Kevin
Marshall, Jack
Mehlman, Bruce
Quintero, Richard
Sade, Mike

Defense:
Adolphi, Ronald
Carey, Rob
DePalma, Evelyn
Groeber, Ginger
Rider, Melissa
Romney, Lisa

Education:
Burrow, Bill
Cavataio, Tony
Luigart, Craig
Zeiher, Jacqueline

Energy:
Warnick, Walter

Environmental Protection Agency:
Nelson, Kimberly
Shaw, Denice

Federal Emergency Management Agency:
Jones, Yolanda

Federal Energy Regulatory Commission:
Russo, Tom

Federal Reserve Bank:
Madine, Charles

General Services Administration:
Barr, Marcerto
Boddie, Tisha

Diaz, Deborah
Dorris, Martha
Freebairn, Tom
Gross, Tanya
Koses, Jeffrey
Mitchell, Mary
Murphy, Roxie
Petersen-Parker, Wanda
Royal, Marion
Sindelar, John
Taylor, Ron
Timchak, Steve
Temoshok, David
Thurston, Keith

Health and Human Services:
Godesky, Doug
Mahaney, Steve
Markovitz, Paul
Reester, Heidi
Roach, Joseph
Williams, Maureen

Housing and Urban Development:
Eden, Donna

Interior:
Brownell, Peter
Haycock, Bob
Lesher, Sky
Mahoney, John

Justice:
Evans, Karen
Hutchinson, Selena
McElhaney, Bill

Labor:
Moritz, Russell

National Aeronautics Space Administration:
Holcombe, Lee
Stepka, Ken

National Endowment for the Humanities:
Bobley, Brett

Nuclear Regulatory Commission:
Clayman, Lew

Cudd, Karen

Office of Management and Budget:
Basile, Julie
Chenok, Daniel
Forman, Mark
Frater, Anthony
McVay, William
Seehra, Jasmeet
Springer, Edward
Swab, Sandy
White, Kamela
Williams, Jerry
Womer, Jonathan

Small Business Administration:
Nillson, Ernst

Social Security Administration:
Trenkle, Tony

State:
Sheerin, Dan

Transportation:
Mercier, Larry.
Powers-King, M.
Preston, Phyllis

Treasury:
Arnold, Jo Lynn
Canales, Mayi
Fletcher, Jackie
Kotelnicki, Donna
Curry, Bernadette

US Agency for Internal Development:
Mazer, Bernie
Tashjian, Steve

Veteran's Administration:
Russell, Lois

Appendix C: Task Force Process

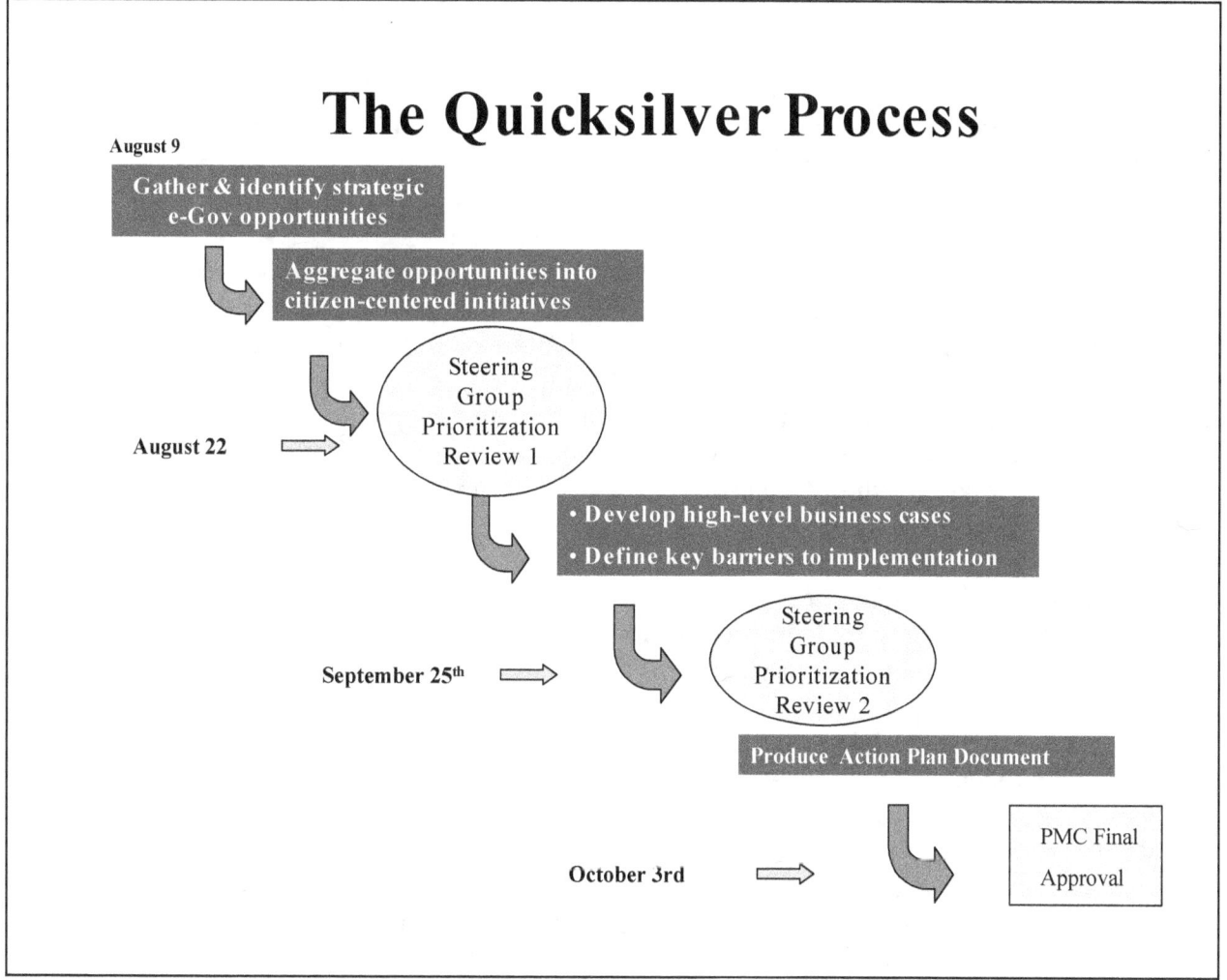

Figure C-1: *An Overview of the "Quicksilver Process" Used by the Task Force.*

Appendix D. Initiative Summaries

Government to Citizen

Recreation One-Stop
Proposed Agency Managing Partner: DOI

This initiative will build upon "Recreation.gov" and will provide a one-stop, searchable database of recreation areas nationwide, featuring online mapping and integrated transactions, including online campground reservations and the purchase of recreational passes, maps and other products. The project will include links to recreational opportunities provided by all levels of government.

Value to Citizen: A single source of information through a simpler and more user-friendly site will reduce search time and provide better service to citizens. The value of the service will increase through more detailed information and the ability to conduct transactions online. Users will be able to find information and conduct transactions at a single site, rather than searching through multiple agency Web sites.

Value to the Government: Through reduced duplication, increased sales and employee timesavings, this project should save federal agencies approximately $5 million annually in avoided costs.

Eligibility Assistance Online
Proposed Agency Managing Partner: Labor

Through a common Internet portal, citizens (with a focus on high-need demographic groups) will have an online tool for identifying government benefit programs from which they may be eligible to receive assistance.

Value to Citizen: Each citizen attempting to determine benefits eligibility should save approximately 50 minutes by using this service over current services. Citizens can also learn about benefits they were eligible to receive but might not know about.

Value to the Government: Customer service calls will be reduced by approximately 750,000 a year, and the government will save approximately $4 million a year through eliminating redundancy.

Online Access for Loans
Proposed Agency Managing Partner: Education

The Online Access for Loans initiative allows citizens and businesses to find the loan programs that meet their needs.

Value to Citizen: Citizens will have faster, easier access to loan information and transactions.

Value to the Government: Employees will save time in managing the loan process.

USA Services
Proposed Agency Managing Partner: GSA

The USA Service initiative will use best practices in customer relationship management to enable citizens to quickly obtain service online, while improving responsiveness and consistency across government agencies.   This initiative would enable citizens to personalize the combination of services they obtain across multiple programs and agencies in a privacy-protected environment.

Value to Citizen: More timely and helpful customer service and more consistent customer service across lines of communication and government programs.

Value to the Government: Redundancy of operation will be eliminated across agencies and employees will save time operating customer relationship management tools.

EZ Tax Filing
Proposed Agency Managing Partner: Treasury/IRS

The initiative would make it easier for citizens to files taxes in a Web-enabled environment.

Value to Citizen: Citizens will no longer have to pay for basic, automated tax preparation. Refund checks will be delivered sooner, online security will be increased and customer service will be improved.

Value to the Government: More information is delivered electronically, reducing data errors. A higher percentage of tax forms are filled out correctly, reducing customer follow-up. Call center receives fewer calls, reducing staffing costs.

Government to Business

Online Rulemaking Management
Proposed Agency Managing Partner: DOT

This initiative would provide access to the rulemaking process for citizens anytime, anywhere. An existing "e-Docket" system would be expanded and enhanced to serve as a government-wide system for agency dockets. Other agency systems would use the system by creating "storefronts" consistent with statutory requirements for each agency under the Administrative Procedures Act. Comments would be organized using knowledge management tools to improve the quality of rules.

Value to Citizen: A single portal for businesses and citizens to access the rulemaking process, creating a more collaborative and transparent atmosphere in which to make policy and public safety decisions. It will also improve the quality of policy decision-making by increasing citizen and business participation in the rulemaking process. Public participation is estimated to increase by 600 percent.

Value to the Government: Elimination of duplicative and redundant systems that currently exist or are being developed. Estimated $9.75 million in savings from consolidating space and FTE costs for 57 rulemaking agencies. Without a government-wide e-Docket system, the federal government will expend nearly $1 billion in development and annual operational costs.

Expanding Electronic Tax Products for Businesses
Proposed Agency Managing Partner: Treasury /IRS

This initiative's goals include decreasing the number of tax-related forms that an employer must file, providing timely and accurate tax information to employers, increasing the availability of electronic tax filing and modeling simplified federal and state tax employment laws.

Value to Citizen: Reduce the burden of compliance with tax laws for businesses. Upon implementation, this initiative offers cost savings of up to $182 per year, per small business. Aggregated, small businesses stand to save up to $6.4 billion over six years. Benefits to large and mid-sized companies should be greater as they tend to spend considerably more time and effort on tax preparation.

Value to the Government: Increases the accuracy and reliability of tax data, as well as the costs associated with paper processing. IRS and SSA may save $16 million annually in staff and printing/mailing costs. It also reduces the costs to states for processing wage and tax data by 5.6 percent.

Federal Asset Sales
Proposed Agency Managing Partner: GSA
Prospective customers will be able to find assets that they are interested in, regardless of the agency that holds those assets. Customers will be able to bid and/or make purchases electronically for financial, real and disposable assets.

Value to Citizen: The creation of a single, easy-to-find point of access, rather than 150 disparate sites, will lower transaction costs and make it easier to do business with the government.

Value to the Government: An estimated $15 million may be saved by consolidating 150 federal Web sites. Additional potential cost savings of approximately $750 million annually associated with the costs of excess building space could be achieved.

International Trade Process Streamlining
Proposed Agency Managing Partner: DOC
The initiative would create a single customer-focused site where new or existing exporters could be assisted electronically through the entire export process. The 20 current Web sites would be organized and accessed through a single entry point.

Value to Citizen: The average export transaction by small to medium exporters (SME) is $400,000. If 224,000 SMEs increase even by a small amount, exports might increase by a billion dollars or more.

Value to the Government: Could streamline 19 agencies involved in trade promotion.

One-Stop Business Compliance Information
Proposed Agency Managing Partner: SBA
This initiative would provide information on laws and regulations that can help users understand compliance information. It would also offer wizards and tutorials to help users determine if rules apply to them and how to proceed. To the maximum extent possible, permits would be completed, submitted and approved online.

Value to Citizen: Currently, the regulatory burden on small business is $7,000 per employee. The creation of a single, cross-agency, business compliance portal will reduce the regulatory burden on the private sector.

Value to the Government: Streamlined business processes and economies of scale would reduce agency costs for achieving business compliance. Government-wide savings of an estimated $10 to $20 million could be realized after full implementation. Additional savings would be realized as a result of staff reductions from online permitting.

Consolidated Health Informatics (business case)
Proposed Agency Managing Partner: HHS
The initiative would provide the basis for a simplified and unified system for sharing and reusing medical record information among government agencies and their private healthcare providers and insurers. It would enable a single mechanism for making those records accessible.
Value to Citizen: Reduce private sector healthcare expenditures for administration (accounts for $57 billion) and improve healthcare for one-half of the population of the United States.
Value to the Government: Order of magnitude savings (from days to minutes) are possible in the area of managing, transporting, copying and exchanging paper medical records. Upon full implementation, this initiative could result in savings of up to $100 million.

Government to Government

Geospatial Information One-Stop
Proposed Agency Managing Partner: DOI
The Geospatial Information One-Stop will provide access to the federal government's spatial data assets in a single location and help make state and local spatial data assets more accessible. federal agencies will also make their planned and future spatial data activities available to state and local governments to promote collaboration and reduce duplicative efforts. Data standards developed through an intergovernmental process will result in data that can be used multiple times for multiple purposes, saving taxpayer money. It will also help empower the private sector by communicating the characteristics of a desired standardized data product.
Value to Citizen: Standardized and reliable spatial data can help save hundreds of millions of dollars annually through consolidation and coordination of spatial data acquisition and maintenance. It will reduce search time for geospatial assets from weeks to minutes. Lastly, it can help improve and expedite citizen service by making data more readily available to agencies requiring that information to perform their governmental functions.
Value to the Government: Full deployment will result in easier, more reliable access to spatial data that should result in hundreds of millions of dollars saved annually by eliminating redundant data collection and increasing opportunities for cost-sharing partnerships. Consolidation and coordination of spatial data assets are critical enablers for other E-Government initiatives, as well as for the Homeland Security effort.

e-Grants
Proposed Agency Managing Partner: HHS
This initiative will create an electronic grants portal for grant recipients and the grant-making agencies that will streamline, simplify and provide an electronic option for grants management across the government. This effort will include the work of the 26 federal grant-making agencies to implement P.L.106-107.
Value to Citizen: A single grant portal will simplify the application process and increase awareness of grant opportunities resulting in a reduction of time spent preparing and searching for grants.
Value to the Government: Save $1 billion in federal funds currently devoted to the administration of grants. Consolidated Web site will save as much as $20 million in postage costs.

Disaster Assistance and Crisis Response
Proposed Agency Managing Partner: FEMA
This initiative involves a public, one-stop portal containing information from applicable public and private organizations involved in disaster preparedness, response, recovery and mitigation. This portal will also serve as a single point of application for all disaster assistance programs.
Value to Citizen: Accurate and timely data may result in saved lives and reduction in property damage. Tens of millions of dollars will be saved in the reduction of insurance costs and lawsuits. A single point of application for disaster assistance will save time during the application and disbursement process.
Value to the Government: Elimination of redundant programs and administrative costs in agencies that provide disaster assistance.

Wireless Public SAFEty Interoperable COMmunications/ Project SAFECOM
Proposed Agency Managing Partner: Treasury
For public safety officials to be effective in their daily responsibilities, as well as before, during and after an emergency event, public safety agencies throughout all levels of government, i.e. federal, state and local, must be able to communicate with each other. This initiative would address the Nation's critical shortcomings in efforts by public safety agencies to achieve interoperability and eliminate redundant wireless communications infrastructures. At the same time, it would assist state and local interoperability and interoperability between federal public safety networks.
Value to Citizen: Coordinated public safety/law enforcement communication will result in saved lives, as well as better-managed disaster response. Consolidated networks will yield cost savings through reduction in communication devices, management overhead of multiple networks, maintenance and training.
Value to the Government: Billions of dollars could be saved through a right-sized set of consolidated, interoperable federal networks, linked to state wireless networks,

resulting in a reduction in communications infrastructure, overhead, maintenance and training.

e-Vital (business case)
Proposed Agency Managing Partner: SSA

This initiative would expand the existing vital records online data exchange efforts between federal agencies and state governments.

Value to Citizen: Elimination of burden imposed on citizens to obtain and deliver vital record information from local government to the federal government. Enables more efficient and effective benefit qualification.

Value to the Government: Save millions of dollars annually through fraud detection from computer matching programs as well as from reductions in erroneous payments.

Internal Efficiency and Effectiveness

e-Training
Proposed Agency Managing Partner: OPM

The vision is to provide a repository of government-owned courseware to be made available to all governments (federal, state and local), to provide high interest and government-required training to government employees at economies of scale pricing. In addition, this would foster development of communities of practice. This initiative supports achievement of the President's Human Capital initiative.

Value to Citizen: Easy one-stop access to just-in-time training with more effective development and retention of high-quality, diversified work force

Value to the Government: Low-cost delivery of effective training

Recruitment One-Stop
Proposed Agency Managing Partner: OPM

This initiative would improve the federal hiring process by improving the functionality of the federal automated employment information system. It would provide job seekers with streamlined resume submission, online feedback about their status in the employment process and integration with automated assessment tools. The initiative will provide federal employers with a searchable resume database.

Value to Citizen: This process will allow job seekers to enter their resume information once to apply for multiple federal vacancies and to receive up-to-the-minute information regarding the status of their application(s).

Value to the Government: This process will give agencies broader and faster access to resumes and the automated tools needed to select candidates. It makes the government a competitive player with the private sector in the recruitment market.

Enterprise HR Integrations
Integrated Human Resources and e-Clearance
Proposed Agency Managing Partner: OPM
This initiative will eliminate the need for paper employee records, enable strategic decisions regarding the use of human capital and financial resources to improve agency performance and address emerging needs. It will also allow for the electronic transfer of HR data throughout the federal sector, better protect the rights and benefits of the federal workforce and streamline and improve government-wide reporting and data analyses. It will reduce the time required to seek and access employee and contractor security clearance information.
Value to Citizen: Improves services and protects the rights and benefits of the federal workforce and provides faster security clearances.
Value to the Government: Streamlines reporting, reduces dependency on paper-based processes, while improving HR capabilities and communications, all at a lower cost.

e- Payroll/HR (Payroll Processing Consolidation)
Proposed Agency Managing Partner: OPM
The vision is to simplify and unify elements of the Payroll/HR process in order to consolidate and integrate HR and payroll systems across government. This effort will provide several hundred million dollars of savings to organizations and significantly reduce future information technology (IT) investments and could foster direct privatization. This initiative supports achievement of the five dimensions of the President's Management Agenda.
Value to Citizen: A government that works more efficiently is one that better serves its citizens.
Value to the Government: Allows the federal government to consolidate payroll operations to simplify and unify processes, thus saving dollars that would be spent on multiple facilities, systems and management.

e-Travel
Proposed Agency Managing Partner: GSA
Agencies will use a common travel management system throughout the federal government. Existing travel management resources will be consolidated and processes will be simplified for cheaper, more efficient operation.
Value to Citizen: One-stop integrated travel services for all federal employees
Value to the Government: Reduced cycle time and improved travel and budget information at a lower cost.

Integrated Acquisition Environment
Proposed Agency Managing Partner: GSA
Agencies will begin sharing common data elements to enable other agencies to make more informed procurement, logistical, payment and performance assessment decisions. It will also allow agencies to make maximum use of E-market approaches.
Value to Citizen: Cost savings to the taxpayer based on a more effective process that leverages scale with more supplier opportunities.
Value to the Government: Will make the purchase of goods and services faster and less expensive, while providing more access to small business.

Electronic Records Management
Proposed Agency Managing Partner: NARA
This initiative will provide the tools that agencies will need to manage their records in electronic form, addressing specific areas of electronic records management where agencies are having major difficulties. This project will provide guidance on electronic records management applicable government-wide and will provide tools for agencies to transfer electronic records to NARA in a variety of data types and formats so that they may be preserved in for future use by the government and citizens.
Value to Citizen: Easier process for creating information, with more reliable storage, that is also in compliance with the Federal Records Act
Value to the Government: More efficient operations that meet the statutory requirements of the Federal Records Act.

<u>Initiatives That Address Barriers to E-Government Success</u>

e-Authentication
Proposed Agency Managing Partner: GSA (Infrastructure)
e-Authentication will build and enable the mutual trust needed to support wide spread use of electronic interactions between the public and government and across governments. This will establish a method for satisfactorily establishing 'identity,' without which the promise of E-Government will never reach its full potential. The project will establish common interoperable authentication solutions for all of the E-Government initiatives.
Value to Citizen: Secure, consistent method of proving identity to the federal government.
Value to the Government: Eliminate redundancy in electronic signature technology and policy operations, thereby reducing costs and employee time required.

Federal Architecture
Proposed Agency Managing Partner: OMB
This activity, which supports all of the initiatives, will map government processes by line of business. It will develop information, data and application interface standards to eliminate redundancies and yield improved operating efficiency and effectiveness.
Value to Citizen: Citizens are best served by an efficient and effective government.
Value to the Government: A well architected federal information system will provide a more efficient and effective government by eliminating redundancies.

www.ingramcontent.com/pod-product-compliance
Lightning Source LLC
Chambersburg PA
CBHW080640290526
45790CB00007B/3150